FAST FOR

ROBOTS

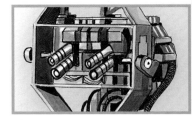

Artist and Author:

Mark Bergin studied at Eastbourne College of Art and has specialised in historical reconstructions, aviation, maritime and hi-tech subjects since 1983. He has been commissioned by aerospace companies and has illustrated a number of books on flight and space, including **Space Shuttle** and **Exploration of Mars** in the *Fast Forward* series. He lives in Bexhill-on-Sea, England, with his wife and three children.

Series creator:

David Salariya was born in Dundee, Scotland, where he studied illustration and printmaking. He has illustrated a wide range of books and has created many new series of books for publishers in the U.K. and overseas. In 1989 he established The Salariya Book Company. He lives in Brighton with his wife, the illustrator Shirley Willis, and their son Jonathan.

Consultant:

Peter Turvey studied Physics and Astronomy at the University of Leicester and History of Technology at Imperial College London. Working at the Science Museum, London, he has been involved in a wide range of projects including the Space and Challenge of Materials galleries and a computerised Visitor Information Network. He has also worked on a wide range of books on technology. He lives in Middlesex with his wife and two children.

Editor:

Karen Barker Smith

Assistant Editor:

Stephanie Cole

Created, designed and produced by
THE SALARIYA BOOK COMPANY LTD
25 Marlborough Place,
Brighton BN1 1UB

Published in Great Britain in 2001 by
Hodder Wayland, an imprint of
Hodder Children's Books

A catalogue record for this book is available
from the British Library.

ISBN 0 7502 3624 8

Printed in China

Hodder Children's Books
A division of Hodder Headline Ltd
338 Euston Road, London NW1 3BH

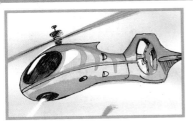

ROBOTS

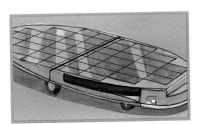

Written and illustrated by
MARK BERGIN

Created and designed by
DAVID SALARIYA

W
HODDER
Wayland

An imprint of Hodder Children's Books

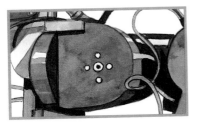

Contents

6

What are Robots?

The origins of robot designs, from the
fantastic to the realistic.

8

Single-Function Robots

Robots designed to perform repetitive tasks
rapidly and accurately.

10

Robots in Hazardous Situations

Bomb disposal, undersea and other robots
designed to enter situations too dangerous
for human involvement.

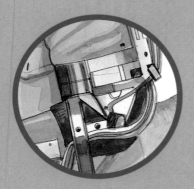

14

Robots in the Film Industry

Robotic characters and creatures used for
our entertainment.

16

Artificial Intelligence

The development of robots that can think
for themselves.

20

Robo-Docs
Robots designed to assist in surgery and other medical procedures.

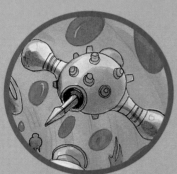

23

Nanorobots
The miniaturised future of medical treatment.

24

Robots in Space
Robots at work all around our solar system.

28

Robots for the Future
The rapid advances in technology that are bringing amazing futuristic robot designs closer to reality.

30

Glossary

31

Robot Facts

32

Index

What are Robots?

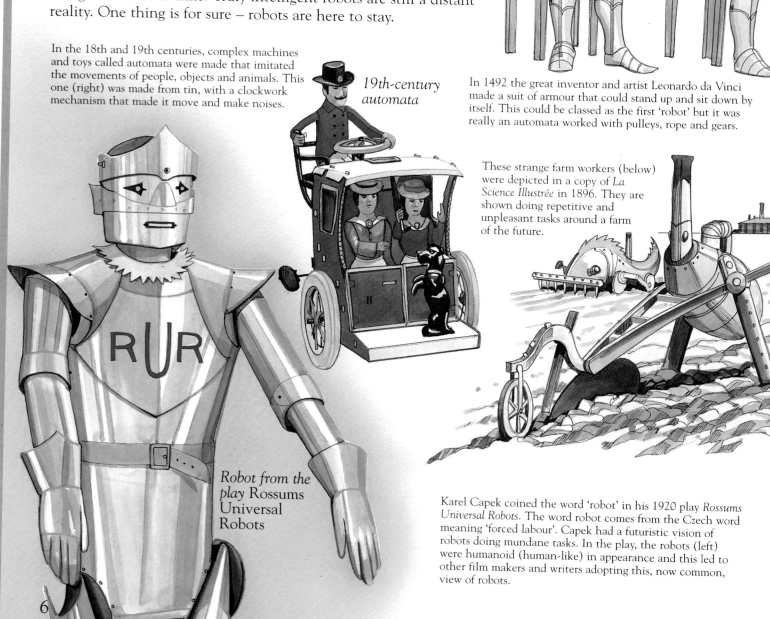

Leonardo da Vinci's suit of armour 'robot'

Across the world, there are millions of robots working around the clock. They carry out a variety of tasks with consistency and accuracy and have freed people from many types of monotonous, dangerous or unpleasant work. Robots are difficult to define. They are mechanical devices that perform human-like actions, but not many robots look human. A welding robot on a car production line does not need legs to perform its job, for example. Most robots are designed for their particular task, whether it be working on the bottom of the ocean or the surface of Mars and it is this that governs what they look like. Some robots can climb, walk, catch, balance, sense objects and even recognise faces. Despite the presence of hundreds of forms of robots in action today, the study of robotics is still in its early stages and new developments are being made all the time. Truly intelligent robots are still a distant reality. One thing is for sure – robots are here to stay.

In the 18th and 19th centuries, complex machines and toys called automata were made that imitated the movements of people, objects and animals. This one (right) was made from tin, with a clockwork mechanism that made it move and make noises.

19th-century automata

In 1492 the great inventor and artist Leonardo da Vinci made a suit of armour that could stand up and sit down by itself. This could be classed as the first 'robot' but it was really an automata worked with pulleys, rope and gears.

These strange farm workers (below) were depicted in a copy of *La Science Illustrée* in 1896. They are shown doing repetitive and unpleasant tasks around a farm of the future.

Robot from the play Rossums Universal Robots

Karel Capek coined the word 'robot' in his 1920 play *Rossums Universal Robots*. The word robot comes from the Czech word meaning 'forced labour'. Capek had a futuristic vision of robots doing mundane tasks. In the play, the robots (left) were humanoid (human-like) in appearance and this led to other film makers and writers adopting this, now common, view of robots.

Female robot from the film Metropolis

The 1927 film *Metropolis*, directed by Fritz Lang, was set in a futuristic city in the year 2000. In the film, a female robot (left) becomes 'alive'. The imagery portrayed has been the film industry's inspiration behind creations such as Robbie the Robot in *Lost in Space* and C-3PO in the *Star Wars* films.

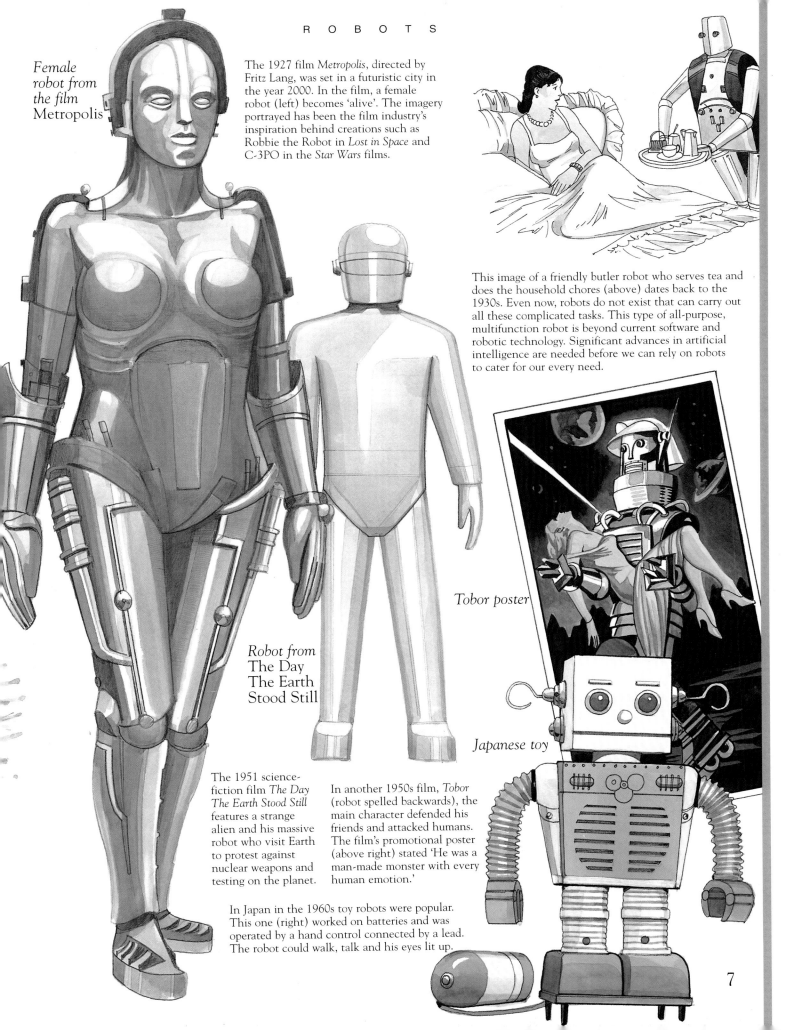

This image of a friendly butler robot who serves tea and does the household chores (above) dates back to the 1930s. Even now, robots do not exist that can carry out all these complicated tasks. This type of all-purpose, multifunction robot is beyond current software and robotic technology. Significant advances in artificial intelligence are needed before we can rely on robots to cater for our every need.

Tobor poster

Japanese toy

Robot from The Day The Earth Stood Still

The 1951 science-fiction film *The Day The Earth Stood Still* features a strange alien and his massive robot who visit Earth to protest against nuclear weapons and testing on the planet.

In another 1950s film, *Tobor* (robot spelled backwards), the main character defended his friends and attacked humans. The film's promotional poster (above right) stated 'He was a man-made monster with every human emotion.'

In Japan in the 1960s toy robots were popular. This one (right) worked on batteries and was operated by a hand control connected by a lead. The robot could walk, talk and his eyes lit up.

7

Single-Function Robots

T he first automated production lines using robots started operation in the 1960s. In many types of manufacturing, robots are used for the most repetitive tasks. Robots don't get bored of tedious work or tired and so can perform the same task again and again with total accuracy, day and night.

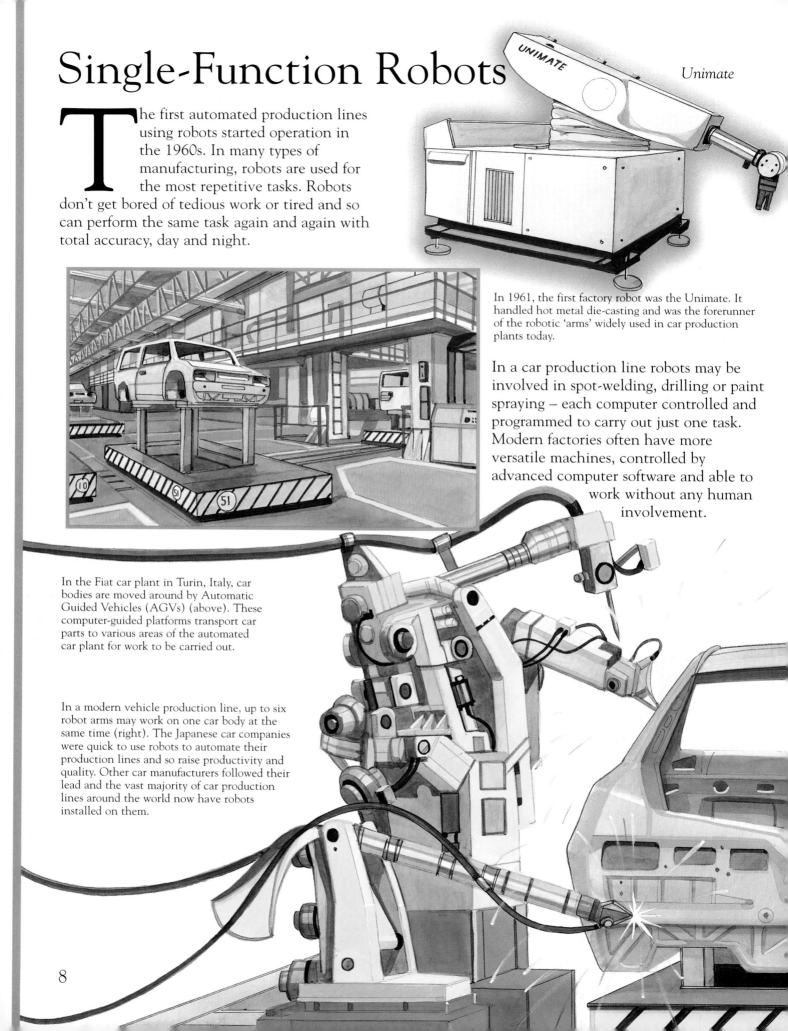

In 1961, the first factory robot was the Unimate. It handled hot metal die-casting and was the forerunner of the robotic 'arms' widely used in car production plants today.

In a car production line robots may be involved in spot-welding, drilling or paint spraying – each computer controlled and programmed to carry out just one task. Modern factories often have more versatile machines, controlled by advanced computer software and able to work without any human involvement.

In the Fiat car plant in Turin, Italy, car bodies are moved around by Automatic Guided Vehicles (AGVs) (above). These computer-guided platforms transport car parts to various areas of the automated car plant for work to be carried out.

In a modern vehicle production line, up to six robot arms may work on one car body at the same time (right). The Japanese car companies were quick to use robots to automate their production lines and so raise productivity and quality. Other car manufacturers followed their lead and the vast majority of car production lines around the world now have robots installed on them.

The first fully automated department store in the world is in Seibu, Japan. Robot shopping trolleys (right) follow customers around using ultrasound to judge their position in the shop and therefore find their way.

Robot shopping trolley

Hospital carers of the future could use robots like Helpmate (left). It is a robotic meals trolley that can also perform basic medical tasks, such as taking patients' blood pressure. It is pre-programmed with a map of the hospital layout and uses ultrasound as a guidance system.

Helmate

Cybermotion SR2

US Cybermotion SR2 is a security robot used in the Los Angeles County Museum in the USA. Cybermotion uses sensors to check for smoke, fire, gas and changes in humidity. It is pre-programmed with a map of the museum and is free to move around without cables or tracks, communicating with a central computer via radio links.

Robot vacuum cleaner

Robot lawnmower

There are single function robots available for the home. This robot lawnmower (above left) is solar powered and senses its way around the lawn. The robot vacuum cleaner (above right) also uses sensors to avoid obstacles. They are both more expensive than normal appliances, but will become cheaper in time.

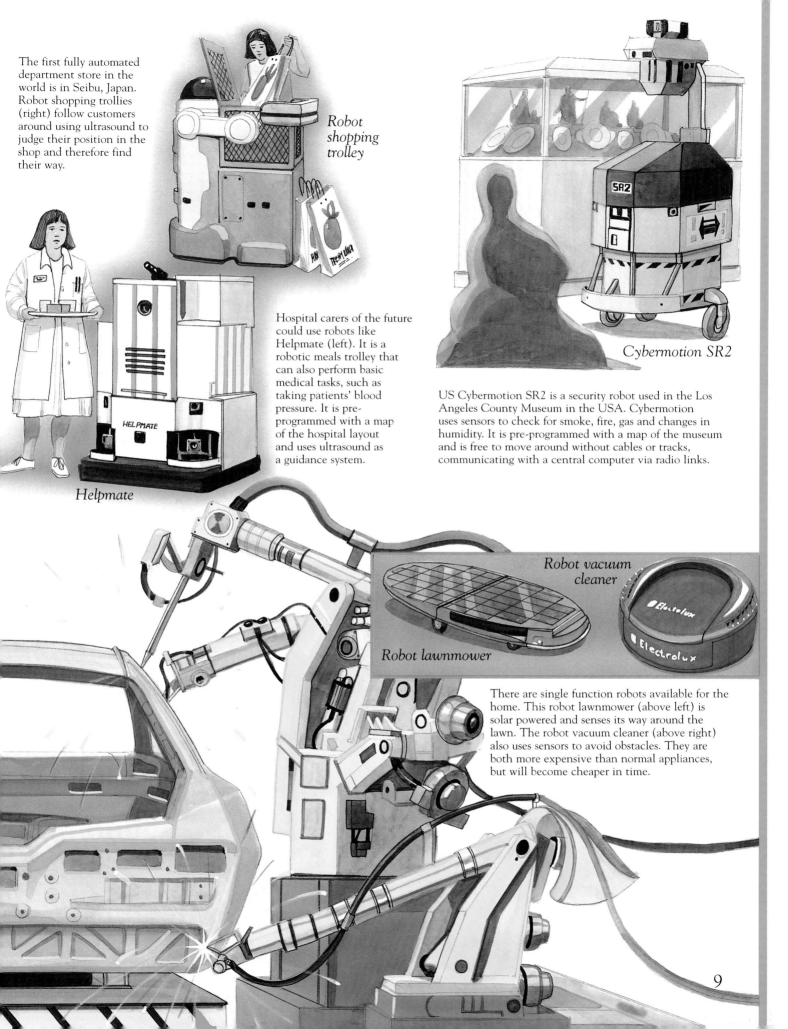

Robots in Hazardous Situations

Areas of intense heat, radioactive contamination, under the sea, extreme pressure or extreme cold are all hazardous environments that particular robots are designed to cope with. In human 'no go' situations like fires, toxic chemical spills, bomb disposals and deep undersea, robots can perform tasks while a human operator monitors or controls them from a safe distance, using equipment such as on-board video cameras.

Robug

The Robug's eight legs, powered by compressed air, give it the ability to walk up walls and across ceilings. Used as a university research testbed, it mimicks the actions of a spider.

Another spider-like robot, Danté II, has been made by NASA. This three-metre high explorer scrambled over an Alaskan volcano called Mount Spurr in 1994 while controlled by technicians over 3,000 km away in California. The robot was developed as part of research into future space probe designs.

Danté II

From the safety of their own vehicle, operators can use radio control to position a bomb disposal 'robot'. These types of machines are not truly robots because they are not automatic or computer controlled. The study of remote-controlled 'robots' is called telerobotics.

The bomb disposal 'robot' can be directed to remove a suspect object from a car. The robot is equipped with two sets of video cameras, a robotic arm with grippers, and rubber-tracked wheels for manoeuvrability and grip. It can either try to defuse the bomb or set off a controlled explosion.

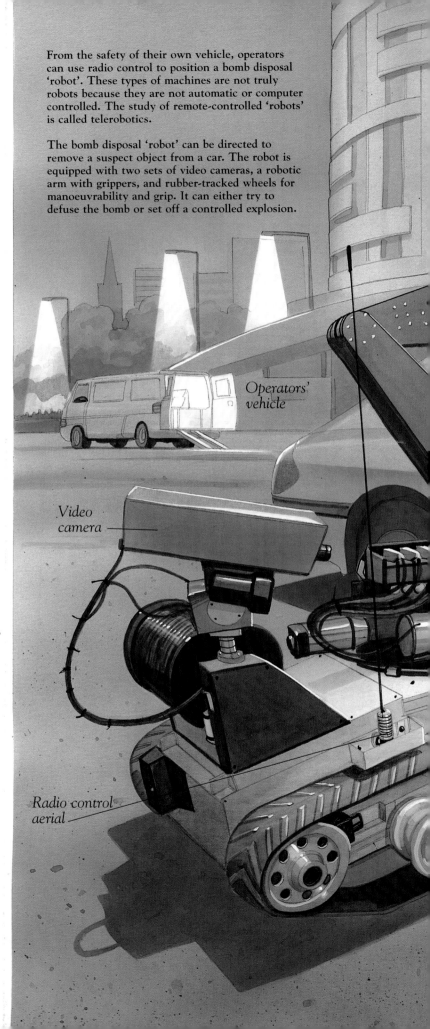

Operators' vehicle

Video camera

Radio control aerial

Video camera

Spotlight

Robotic arm
with grippers

If the 'robot' catches fire,
extinguishers will function
automatically. Machines like
this are regularly used in
areas of conflict and terrorist
activity all around the world.

Rubber tracked wheels

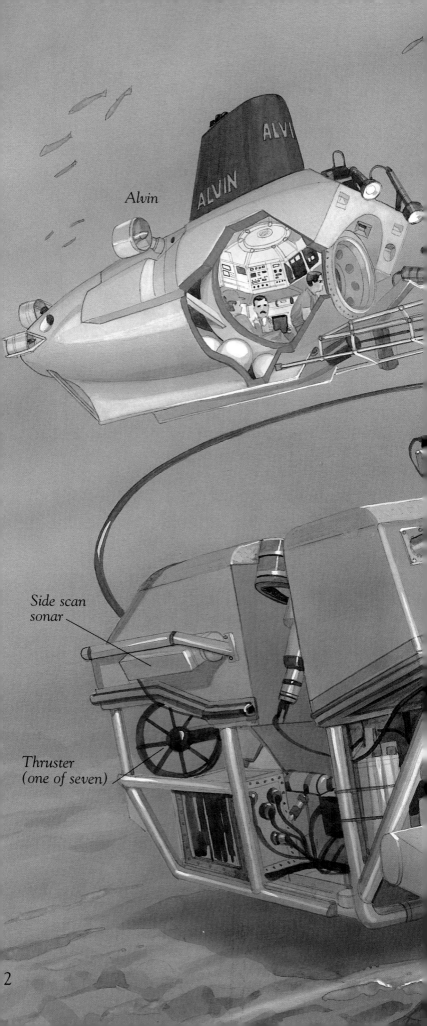

Alvin

Side scan
sonar

Thruster
(one of seven)

One of the most extreme environments robots can work in is that of the ocean floor. At a depth of 1,000 m, water presses on an object around 100 times as much as air does above water. *Jason Junior* is a state-of-the-art underwater robot that can withstand high pressure and can dive to 61,000 m deep. *Jason Jr.* can be launched and controlled from a research ship on the surface, or as a 'swimming eye', attached by a 80 m tether to the submersible *Alvin*. In 1985, the crew of *Alvin* discovered the site of the wreck of *Titanic*. They were able to guide *Jason Jr.* down the stairways inside the huge sunken liner to see what was left of the interior, a place no one had set eyes on since the ship sank in the Northern Atlantic in 1912.

Jason Jr. can be fitted with *Knuckles*, a robotic arm that can pick up objects from the seabed. It brought up amphorae (Greek pots) from the wreck of the ancient Greek trading ship *Isis* in 1989.

80 m of cable attaches Jason Jr. to Alvin

Knuckles – robotic arm with gripper

Jason Junior

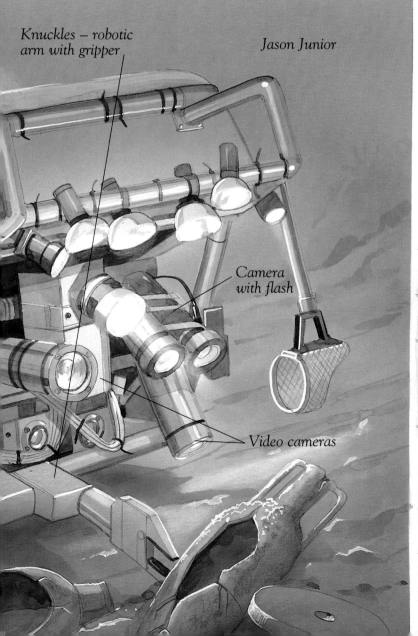

Camera with flash

Video cameras

New robots are currently being designed for fire-fighting and use in the nuclear industry. In the future, the use of fire-fighting robots may become commonplace. They could go straight to the seat of a fire and extinguish it with water and foam without the need for humans to enter such a dangerous situation.

Below, a modern remote controlled fire-fighting robot is being tested in trials. It has already been used in real fires and is especially effective in dealing with chemical and petrol fires. It is constructed from heat resistant materials and has grippers for picking up burning objects.

Robots made of composites (like Kevlar) and metal are not affected by exposure to radiation and are used extensively in the nuclear industry for processing radioactive materials. They can be directed to accurately and safely pick up dangerous objects. These robotic machines are needed to help in the decommission of old and redundant nuclear processing plants.

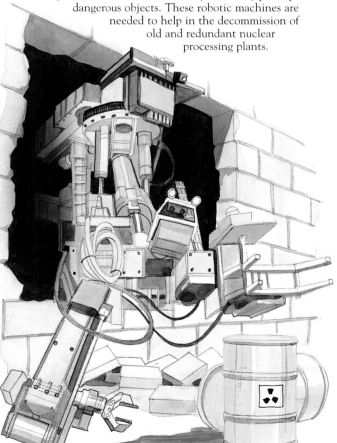

Robots in the Film Industry

Many robot characters have become Hollywood stars, like Robbie the Robot from the film *Forbidden Planet* in the 1950s. In the modern film industry the majority of visual trickery is done with hi-tech computer graphics and animation. But robot 'stand-ins', or animatronics, are still used for close up work to recreate alien creatures, massive dinosaurs or futuristic robots themselves.

The robot playing table-tennis (below) is really a 'master-slave' type machine. Each movement made by the operator is repeated by the robot. Sensors on a framework attached to the operator, also known as a telemetry suit, calculate his every move. This data is then relayed via a computer, Sarcos, to the robot. Sarcos is a very powerful computer the size of a filing cabinet.

Robot operator

Sarcos

Telemetry suit

This nine-tonne model of a Tyrannosaurus Rex is guided by its operator wearing a telemetry suit (below and right). The telemetry suit makes the robotic model do exactly what the operator does. This one controls the model's limbs, head and neck and was used in Steven Spielberg's film, *The Lost World*.

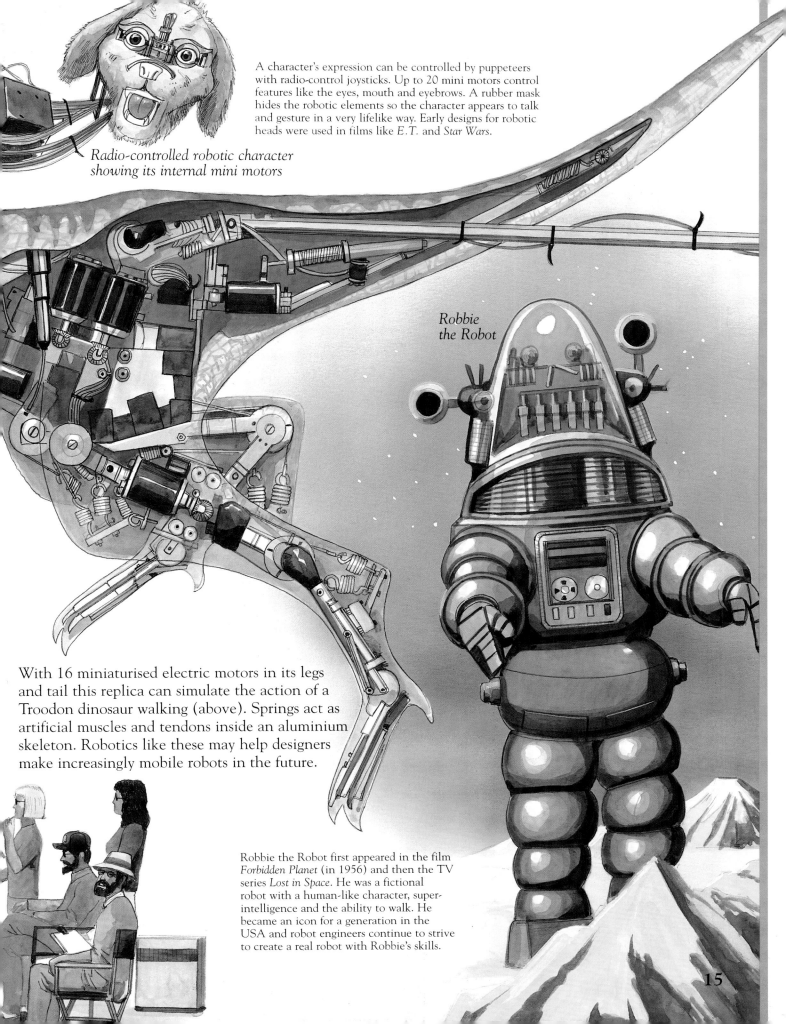

A character's expression can be controlled by puppeteers with radio-control joysticks. Up to 20 mini motors control features like the eyes, mouth and eyebrows. A rubber mask hides the robotic elements so the character appears to talk and gesture in a very lifelike way. Early designs for robotic heads were used in films like *E.T.* and *Star Wars*.

Radio-controlled robotic character showing its internal mini motors

Robbie the Robot

With 16 miniaturised electric motors in its legs and tail this replica can simulate the action of a Troodon dinosaur walking (above). Springs act as artificial muscles and tendons inside an aluminium skeleton. Robotics like these may help designers make increasingly mobile robots in the future.

Robbie the Robot first appeared in the film *Forbidden Planet* (in 1956) and then the TV series *Lost in Space*. He was a fictional robot with a human-like character, super-intelligence and the ability to walk. He became an icon for a generation in the USA and robot engineers continue to strive to create a real robot with Robbie's skills.

15

The teamwork shown by worker ants has inspired scientists to imitate them, programming numbers of small, simple robots to work together without using complex software.

Artificial Intelligence

The aim of all artificial intelligence (AI) research is to develop machines that can think and act without any outside intervention. Artificially intelligent robots can recover from mistakes and work out solutions to problems themselves, becoming more self-sufficient and adapting to changing situations.

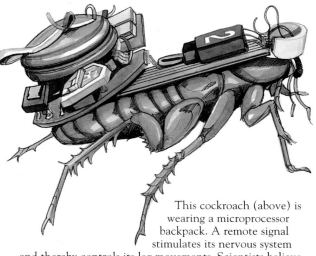

This cockroach (above) is wearing a microprocessor backpack. A remote signal stimulates its nervous system and thereby controls its leg movements. Scientists believe that by studying insect movements they may learn how to make robot legs walk as efficiently as theirs.

Programmed to seek light and react to a light source, these electronic 'ladybirds' developed for research automatically turn to face the sun. They have light-sensitive eyes and are solar powered.

The Department of Cybernetics at the University of Reading, England, is carrying out exciting research into smart robots. Smart robots can communicate with each other without human intervention. The robot pictured (right) is one of seven 'dwarfs', small robots that can perform different types of behaviour. They are pre-programmed with an instinct to flock, herd, follow the leader or avoid each other. Each robot has an infrared transmitter that sends out a unique signal that the other robots can identify. Ultrasound transmitters are used to detect and avoid obstructions as the robots move around.

Illuminated box

Swarm robots

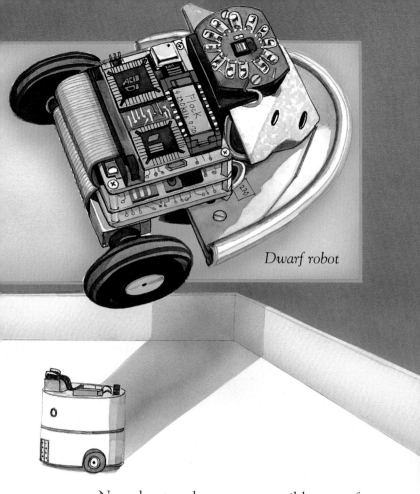

Dwarf robot

Neural networks are one possible way of making thinking machines. They are good at controlling systems. Progress in neural networking has accelerated since the 1980s with huge advances in computer software. Neural networking is a simplified form of the way a human brain works. Things are learned through trial and error and patterns of behaviour can be recognised, even up to the point of predicting future situations and potential problems.

AI researchers test the abilities of their robot designs by giving them tasks or practical games to do. At the University of Alberta, Canada, simple instruction programs are being experimented with. The swarm of robots pictured have been programmed to push an illuminated circular box towards a light. Each robot works independently and does not communicate with the others. It follows a set of simple instructions such as: turn right; move toward the light; push. In this way, the joint efforts of the robots accomplish the goal. Experiments have also used sound to trigger the robots' movements.

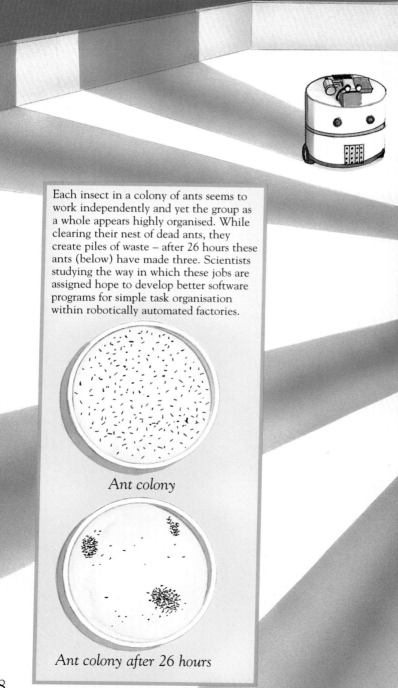

ELMA (Experimental Local Multitasking Arthropod) is a six-legged insect type robot, also developed at the University of Reading, that has been designed to learn how to walk, rather than following instructions. Each leg is controlled independently and has to co-ordinate with the others to make the whole robot move successfully. ELMA has sensors in its aluminium legs that tell the robot when it is making contact with the ground. A radio link enables the robot to communicate with a computer and the data from the leg sensors is used to make a 3D 'map' of ELMA's surroundings. This in turn helps the robot learn from errors it has already made. A central processor or 'brain' in the robot controls the movement of its legs but ELMA has no residual memory – once it is shut down, all it has learned is forgotten.

Each insect in a colony of ants seems to work independently and yet the group as a whole appears highly organised. While clearing their nest of dead ants, they create piles of waste – after 26 hours these ants (below) have made three. Scientists studying the way in which these jobs are assigned hope to develop better software programs for simple task organisation within robotically automated factories.

Ant colony

Ant colony after 26 hours

ELMA

Kismet is an offshoot of the Cog project (see below). A disembodied autonomous robot head, Kismet is a robot with feelings, interacting emotionally with people via its mechanical 'face'. Its creators were influenced by the way a baby learns to communicate with adults. Kismet's facial features can display a range of human emotions: surprise, fear, anger, happiness and even disgust. An audio stereo microphone input is planned, to allow Kismet to hear, along with a synthesized voice, for greater communicative skills.

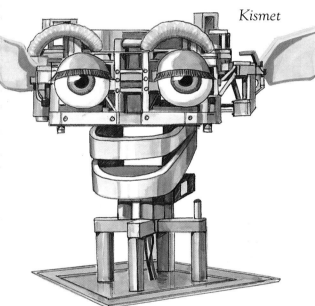

Kismet

Research into humanoid characteristics is leading to the development of robots that can handle objects with much greater sensitivity. Cog is one of these. It has bifocal vision to make locating and picking up objects easier. Sensors detect the size, weight and shape of the object and determine how much pressure is needed to grip it, without either crushing or dropping it.

After each robot in the swarm independently makes a set of simple decisions and movements, together they accomplish the task.

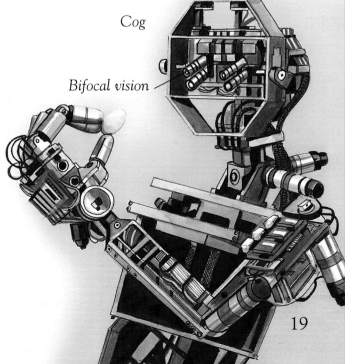

Cog

Bifocal vision

19

Robo-Docs

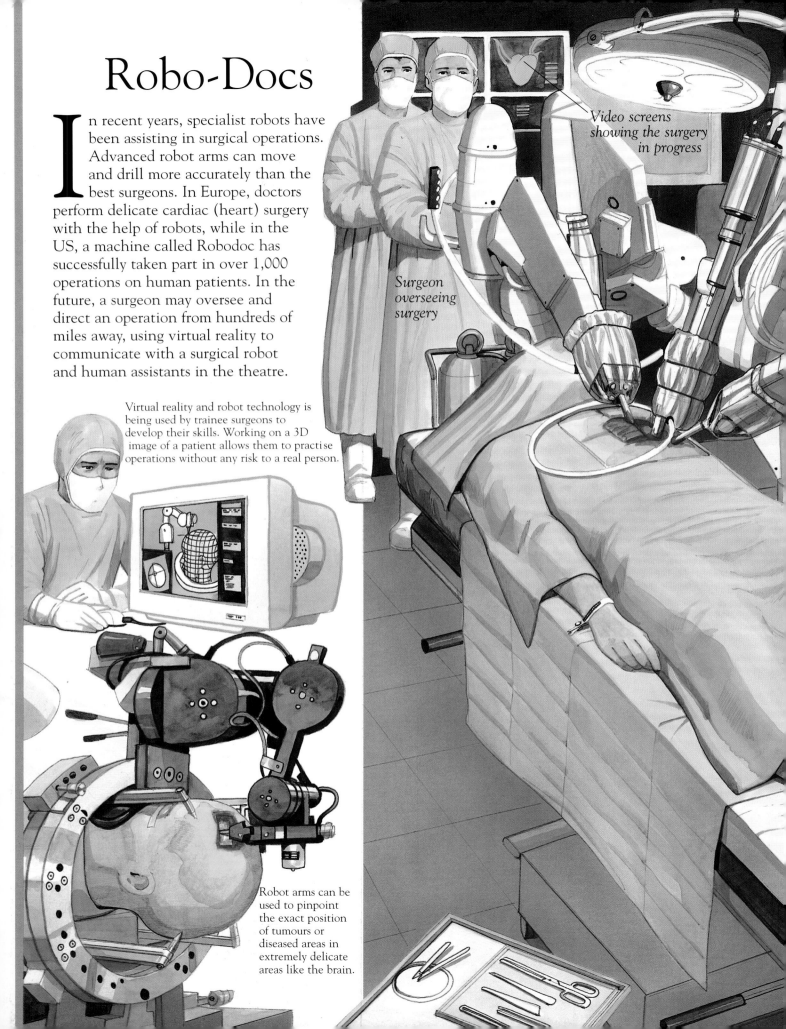

In recent years, specialist robots have been assisting in surgical operations. Advanced robot arms can move and drill more accurately than the best surgeons. In Europe, doctors perform delicate cardiac (heart) surgery with the help of robots, while in the US, a machine called Robodoc has successfully taken part in over 1,000 operations on human patients. In the future, a surgeon may oversee and direct an operation from hundreds of miles away, using virtual reality to communicate with a surgical robot and human assistants in the theatre.

Virtual reality and robot technology is being used by trainee surgeons to develop their skills. Working on a 3D image of a patient allows them to practise operations without any risk to a real person.

Surgeon overseeing surgery

Video screens showing the surgery in progress

Robot arms can be used to pinpoint the exact position of tumours or diseased areas in extremely delicate areas like the brain.

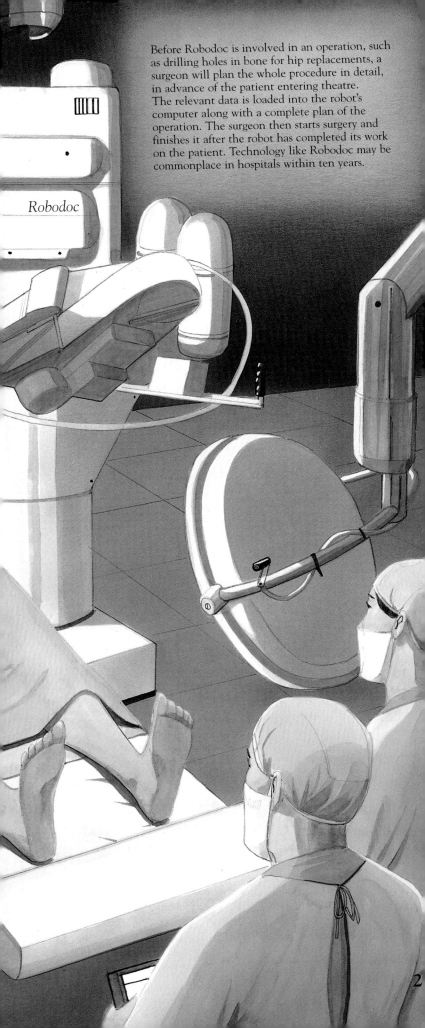

Before Robodoc is involved in an operation, such as drilling holes in bone for hip replacements, a surgeon will plan the whole procedure in detail, in advance of the patient entering theatre. The relevant data is loaded into the robot's computer along with a complete plan of the operation. The surgeon then starts surgery and finishes it after the robot has completed its work on the patient. Technology like Robodoc may be commonplace in hospitals within ten years.

Robodoc

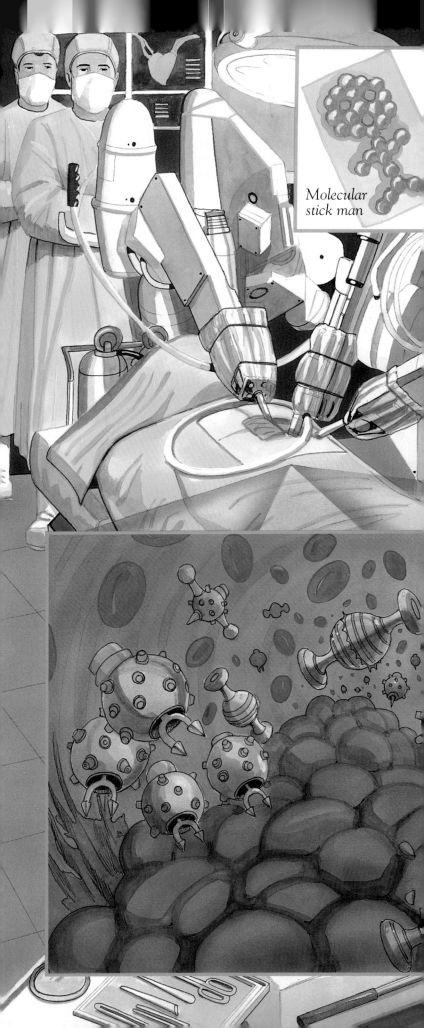

Molecular
stick man

Research into producing working machine parts out of individual atoms is currently taking place. This stick man (far left) was made with only 28 carbon monoxide molecules. Up to 20,000 of these small figures placed in a row would be no wider than a human hair. Computer modelling shows how machine parts may be made at the molecular level (left). Each ball represents one atom – the machine part pictured is just a few nanometres long.

Model of a molecular-sized machine part

Nanorobots

Nanotechnology is robot engineering on the smallest scale. The term comes from the word nanometre, a measurement one thousand millionth of a metre – the width of about ten atoms! In the future, tiny fully working robots could build, repair and clean up around us without us even noticing their existence.

DENSO

DENSO is an inspection robot for factory pipelines. It expands and contracts to move along a pipe, using very little power.

Futuristic nanorobots and probes attack a diseased section of a blood vessel, cleaning it free of cholesterol, unblocking clogged veins and arteries or killing tumours. (left) After the mission is accomplished the nanorobots would either be programmed to biodegrade safely within the patient, or remain in the blood system performing checks like measuring cholesterol levels, blood sugar and hormone levels.

Nanotechnology has other potential applications. Oil slicks could be broken down at a microscopic level and armies of nanorobots could remove pollution from the atmosphere. Even toothpaste full of nanorobots programmed to destroy plaque has been considered! Technology is miniaturising constantly. A fully functional electric motor, only 1.8 mm in size has already been built, so the reality of nanorobots may be just around the corner.

A medical nanorobot of the future may look like this (below). It has incredibly small tools to perform micro-surgery and pumps to dispense drugs into or remove toxins from cells. A tiny communication dish sends and receives ultrasound instructions and data from a medical team outside the patient's body. The outer shell of the nanorobot may be made of diamond which is strong and chemically inert – it would not cause harmful reactions inside a human body.

Nanorobot of the future

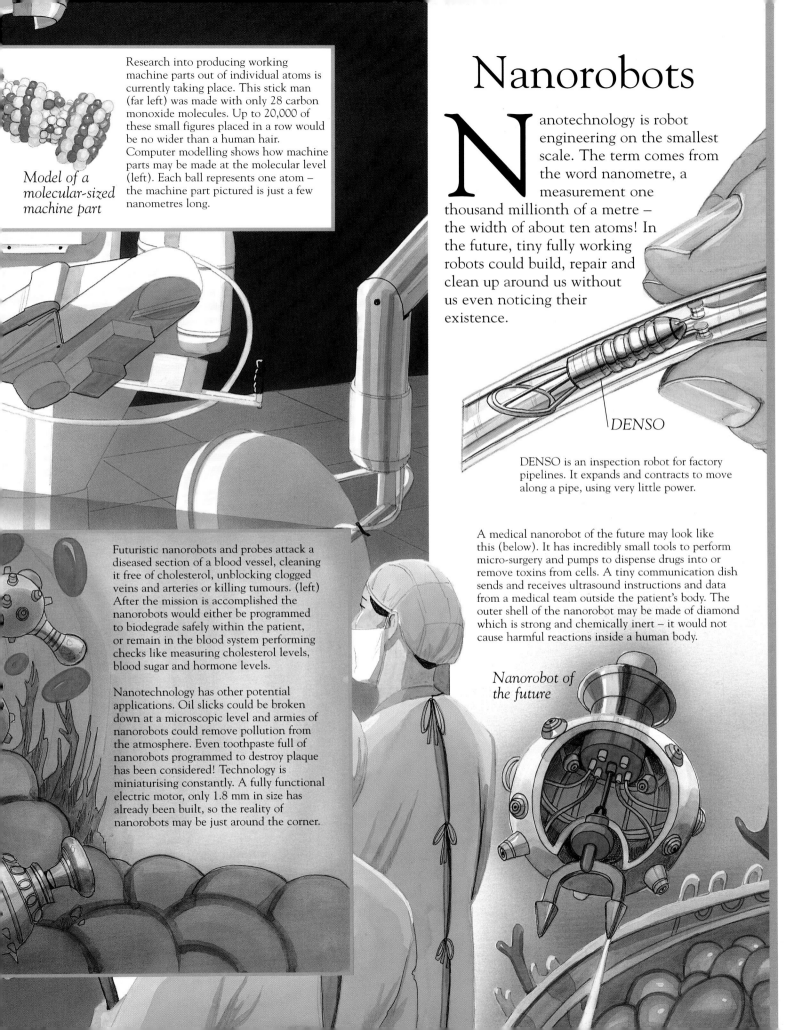

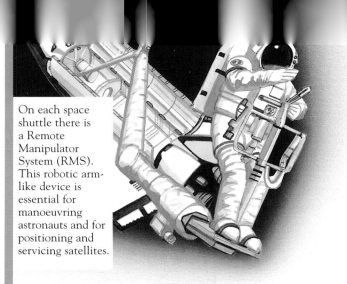

On each space shuttle there is a Remote Manipulator System (RMS). This robotic arm-like device is essential for manoeuvring astronauts and for positioning and servicing satellites.

Sojourner rover

Robots in Space

Unmanned robotic spacecraft are currently exploring parts of the solar system, cheaply and effectively. Human spaceflight is expensive and in many cases not necessary for particular types of research. Space probes like the *Voyager* series have discovered so much, from looking more closely at the moons of Saturn to the high-level bands of cirrus clouds on Neptune. More robotic probes will soon go to Mars, Saturn's largest moon Titan and the surface of a speeding comet, Tempel 1.

This NASA Nomad rover, 1.8 m long, has been developed as a testbed for future unmanned space missions. It has undergone testing in Antarctica and other tough environments. One of these rovers may be sent to the Moon and would be controlled via communications from Earth. It is clever enough to ignore bad or unwise instructions!

NASA Nomad rover

Huygens probe enters Titan's atmosphere

Heat shield separates from probe

The Mars Pathfinder probe landed on the red planet on 4 July 1997 after a seven month and 192 million-km journey from Earth. One day later, the small six-wheeled Sojourner rover started to explore a small area of the planet's rocky surface. The rover became the first wheeled vehicle to land on another planet. It collected surface data with an Alpha Proton X-ray Spectrometer (APXS) to analyse soil and rocks. When the solar powered rover had trouble dealing with obstacles, it stopped to await instructions from mission control.

Saturn

The Huygens probe was built by the European Space Agency (ESA). It will be released to reach Titan, Saturn's largest moon, by November 2004.

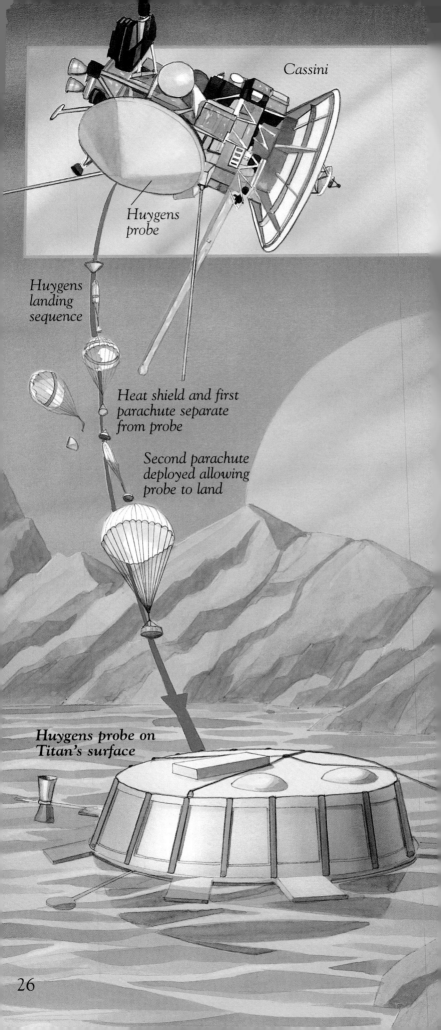

Cassini

Huygens probe

Huygens landing sequence

Heat shield and first parachute separate from probe

Second parachute deployed allowing probe to land

Huygens probe on Titan's surface

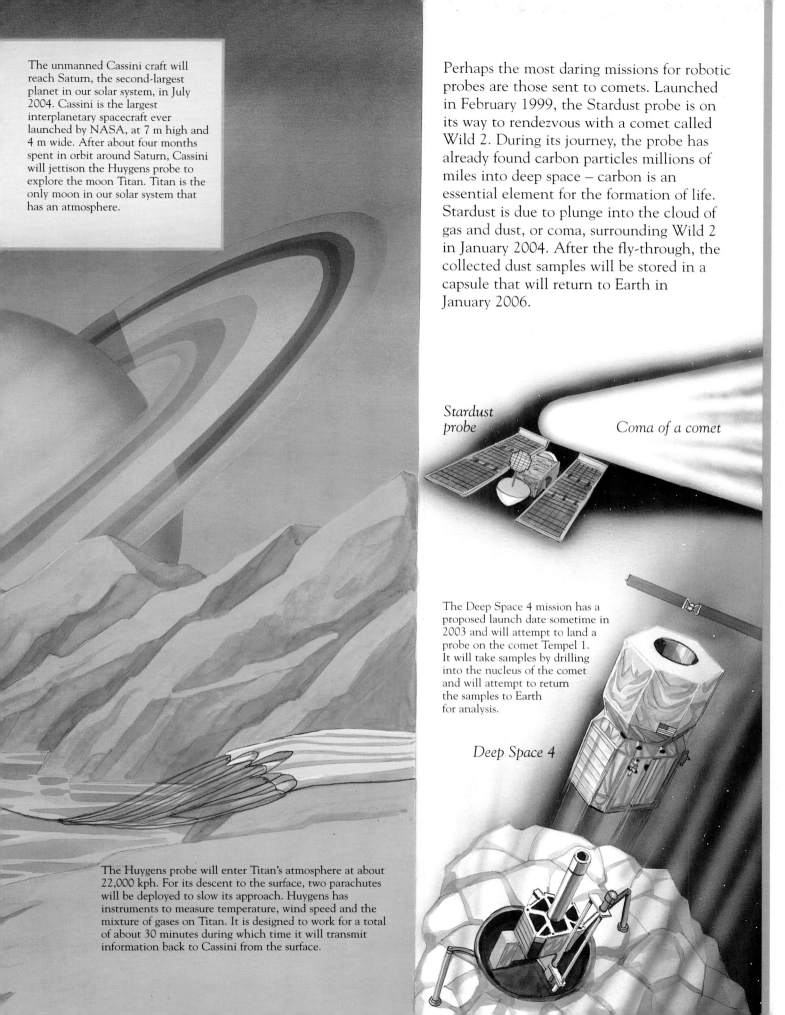

The unmanned Cassini craft will reach Saturn, the second-largest planet in our solar system, in July 2004. Cassini is the largest interplanetary spacecraft ever launched by NASA, at 7 m high and 4 m wide. After about four months spent in orbit around Saturn, Cassini will jettison the Huygens probe to explore the moon Titan. Titan is the only moon in our solar system that has an atmosphere.

Perhaps the most daring missions for robotic probes are those sent to comets. Launched in February 1999, the Stardust probe is on its way to rendezvous with a comet called Wild 2. During its journey, the probe has already found carbon particles millions of miles into deep space – carbon is an essential element for the formation of life. Stardust is due to plunge into the cloud of gas and dust, or coma, surrounding Wild 2 in January 2004. After the fly-through, the collected dust samples will be stored in a capsule that will return to Earth in January 2006.

Stardust probe

Coma of a comet

The Deep Space 4 mission has a proposed launch date sometime in 2003 and will attempt to land a probe on the comet Tempel 1. It will take samples by drilling into the nucleus of the comet and will attempt to return the samples to Earth for analysis.

Deep Space 4

The Huygens probe will enter Titan's atmosphere at about 22,000 kph. For its descent to the surface, two parachutes will be deployed to slow its approach. Huygens has instruments to measure temperature, wind speed and the mixture of gases on Titan. It is designed to work for a total of about 30 minutes during which time it will transmit information back to Cassini from the surface.

Robots for the Future

Technological advances in robotics are being made at an amazing rate. In research laboratories and workshops around the world, robots are being designed that can walk, communicate, swim, pour drinks and recognise sounds, speech and faces. These abilities will eventually make robots commonplace in our daily lives. This century, robots will travel deeper into space to distant comets, planets and moons, work increasingly in factories and on the ocean floor. They will be essential assistants in homes and hospitals. Robots may even form their own communities and evolve, by beginning to design and build improved versions of themselves.

Robot toys and pets may be a common feature in homes of the future. Children's toys, like this robot kit (below), make learning about robotics fun. It has all the main parts of a robot: control motors, grippers and a small computer to program it.

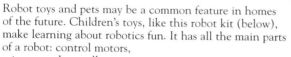

Children's robot kit

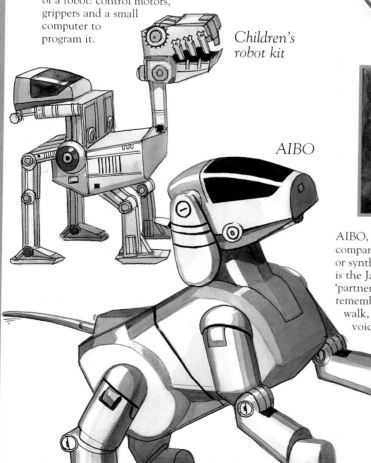

AIBO

The Cypher is an unmanned, military multi-mission reconnaissance and surveillance flying saucer. Only 1.8 m in diameter, it can take off and fly by itself. Only its destination must be provided by the operator.

Cypher

Various designs of microspies

These creations (left and above) are 'microspies' launched using compressed air and flown by remote control The operator uses a hooded viewer to follow the spy's progress. Technological advances and cheaper parts mean that practical use of fly-sized microspies could be a reality this decade.

As technology continues to allow the miniaturisation of more and more items, robot parts are also becoming smaller. These gears and cogs are pictured next to an ant's leg (left)! They were made using technology similar to that used to manufacture microchips. Researchers speculate that in the future, swarms of tiny robot helicopters could be used to keep insect pests under control, making chemical pesticides a thing of the past (below).

AIBO, made by the Japanese company Sony, is a robot pet or synthetic life-form (Aibou is the Japanese word for 'partner' or 'pal'). It can remember its surroundings, walk, sit and respond to voice commands.

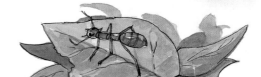

The Predator remote-controlled surveillance aircraft was used in the Bosnian conflict (1991-3) by the US airforce and carried out 128 missions. It uses photographic and infrared images to act as the 'eyes' of a battle group and can fly for over 40 hours at a maximum altitude of 7,600 m.

Darkstar

The Darkstar is an Unmanned Reconnaissance Aerial Vehicle (URAV). This robot aircraft uses stealth technology to cruise at 13,000 m undetected, in all weathers, transmitting close-up images of the ground to soldiers on the battlefield.

Predator

Future unmanned strike aircraft might look like this (below) using highly accurate laser weaponry and stealth technology. These robot craft could use virtual reality to create a 3D picture on computer screen for the operator.

Futuristic unmanned aircraft

Armies of the future may use robotic bugs to cross difficult terrain and drop explosives in enemy positions. Such bugs could also be dropped by aircraft, to land on buildings, enter them and self-detonate.

Futuristic robot bug

By 2020 flying maintenance robots (below) might be monitoring and working on power lines. They could hover and use robotic arms with tools to carry out necessary repairs.

By 2030 it is possible that in every house domestic robots (below) will communicate with a household computer to organise and carry out chores, order shopping and prepare meals.

Robotuna (below) is an underwater vehicle research project, modelled on a blue fin tuna. It is an excellent swimmer, has six motors and a skin made from flexible, stretchy material.

Futuristic domestic robot

Robotuna

Futuristic maintenance robot

Honda-Sapiens

Honda-Sapiens (right) is a humanoid robot that is pushing the boundaries of robot technology. It is the first real robot with the ability to balance, walk up steps and think its way around obstacles or to step over them. It is 1.8 m tall, with an internal battery that lasts 15 minutes before needing to be recharged.

An AUV

Autonomous Underwater Vehicles (AUVs) (left) are submarines can be programmed to independently perform a variety of tasks, such as exploring for gas, oil and mineral deposits. In the future, AUVs could map the seabed, detect environmental hazards and maintain underwater cables and pipelines.

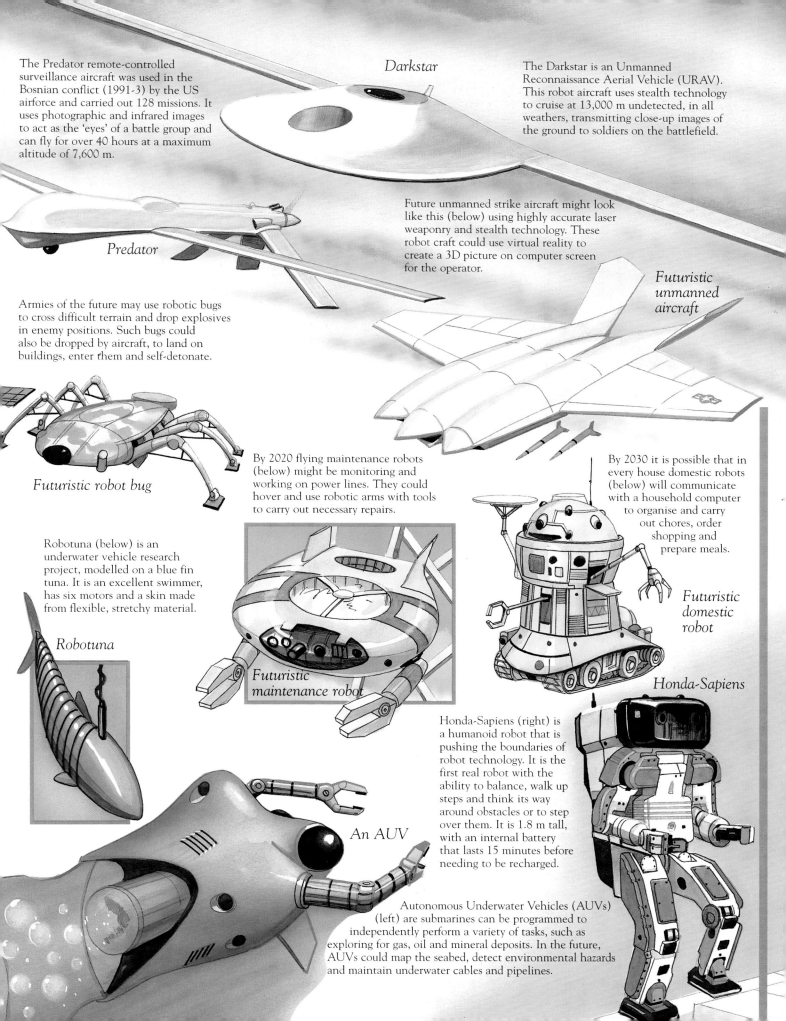

Glossary

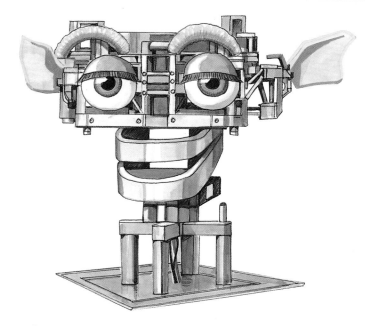

Animatronics
Special-effect models of animals made using robotic techniques, used in films.

Atmosphere
The layer of gases surrounding a planet.

Atom
A term for the smallest particle of a chemical element. It can take part in a chemical reaction or be used to make an object.

Autonomous
A self-governing machine that can make decisions by itself.

Biodegrade
To decompose naturally through the action of bacteria or other living organisms.

Comet
An object, usually made of ice and rock, surrounded by gas, that orbits the sun. A tail sometimes thousands of kilometres long can form when heat causes the 'head' to evaporate.

Decommission
A term used for the removal of radioactive material or contamination from an object or place.

Humanoid
A machine with human qualities or appearance.

Infrared
Light, invisible to the human eye, at the red end of the spectrum.

Interplanetary
Between planets.

Jettison
To release or throw.

NASA
The National Aeronautics and Space Administration – the organization responsible for space research in the United States.

Neural networking
A way of programming computers to perform a great variety of tasks, reflecting the way the complex system of nerves in a human brain works.

Nucleus
The centre of an object around which other parts collect, e.g., the centre of an atom.

Orbit
The curved path an object makes as it travels around another object.

Probe
A robotic device controlled from Earth, designed to explore and study space.

Radio-controlled
Controlled from a distance by radio waves.

Robot
A machine capable of carrying out a complex series of actions automatically, usually controlled by a computer.

Software
The programs and other operating information used in a computer.

Sonar
Sound navigation and ranging. A device used to locate objects underwater by bouncing pulses of sound off them and measuring the time for the echoes to return.

Submersible
A mini-submarine that is launched at sea and recovered again by a specially built mother-ship.

Telerobotics
'Robots' remotely controlled by human operators.

Testbed
Equipment designed specifically for research and development purposes.

Ultrasound
High-frequency sound above the normal range of human hearing.

Robot Facts

The longest robotic arm in use is the Remote Manipulator System (RMS) on the space shuttle. It is 15 m long.

Cybhand is a testbed humanoid hand with three fingers and a thumb. It has tendon-like cables that power electric motors in the fingers to move them.

Autosub 1 is an AUV being developed by Southampton Oceanography Centre, England. It is a data collecting and sampling robot that can operate without human intervention. Seven car batteries provide it with a range of 70 km. Autosub 1 uses a Global Positioning System (GPS) via satellite to calculate its location and sensors provide information on its depth, pitch and roll.

Manny is a humanoid robot used as a testbed for specialist clothing such as protective fire-fighting garments and spacesuits. Manny can simulate breathing and even sweating.

In Tokyo, Japan, a 16-legged spider robot is used to check for cracks in and around gas tanks.

The US remote-controlled surveillance aircraft Predator, is over 8 m long and has a wingspan of nearly 15 m. Four of the aircraft are usually used together for each mission.

There have been several versions of smart robot insects developed by the Department of Cybernetics at the University of Reading, England. Nicknamed the 'seven dwarfs', the first versions were capable of finding their way around an environment using ultrasonic sensors. The second-generation robots were capable of learning, such as how to move and avoid objects. The most recently developed robots can not only learn but also communicate with each other to allow group learning and co-operative behaviour.

Attila is an insect-like robot developed by a research team at the Massachusetts Institute of Technology, USA. It has six legs, 23 motors and 150 sensors. It has the ability to climb and move across rough terrain to perform simple tasks and to repair other machines.

Sprint is a ball-like robotic camera used on the space shuttle. The free-flying robot has 12 thrusters to allow it to move in any direction, at up to 2.7 kph. Its first flight, in November 1997, lasted 76 minutes.

Shear Magic is a robotic arm that shears sheep. It uses ultrasound sensors to gauge the accuracy of its cutting head.

Robart III is a patrol robot used in offices and warehouses. It can deal with intruders by using a six-barrel dart gun that fires tranquilizer darts.

In 1940, science fiction writers Isaac Asimov and John W. Campbell developed laws which state how robots should behave in the future: 1) A robot may not injure a human being or, through inaction, allow a human being to come to harm; 2) A robot must obey the orders given it by human beings except where such orders would conflict with the First Law; 3) A robot must protect its own existence as long as such protection does not conflict with the First or Second Law.

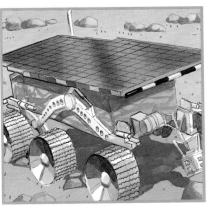

The limitations of current robot technology mean most of them cannot 'see' very well. Shadows and perspective cause problems and they can recognise things only in simple situations.

Danté I was the first spider-like robot built by NASA to investigate live volcanoes. Unfortunately, when it was sent into the crater of Mount Erebus, in Antarctica, it only travelled about 6 m down the crater wall before its tethering cable broke. It tumbled into the volcano, never to be seen again!

Index

Illustrations are shown in **bold** type.

A

AIBO (robotic pet) 28, **28**
Alvin (submersible) 12-13, **12-13**
animation 14
animatronics 14, 30
ants 16, **16**, 18, **18**
artificial intelligence 7, 16-17, 18-19
Asimov, Isaac 31
atmosphere 23, 24, 27, 30
atoms 23, 30
Attila 31
automata 6, **6**
Automatic Guided Vehicles (AGVs) 8, **8**
Autonomous Underwater Vehicles (AUVs) 29, **29**, 31
Autosub 1 31

B

balance 6
bomb disposal 10-11, **10-11**

C

Campbell, John W. 31
Capek, Karel 6
Cassini (spacecraft) 26, 27
Cog (robot) 19, **19**
coma (of a comet) 27, **27**
comets 24, 27, 28, 30
computer graphics 14
computers 8, 9, 14, 18, 21, 23, 28, 29, 30
Cybhand 31
Cypher (robotic aircraft) 28, **28**

D

da Vinci, Leonardo 6
Danté I (robot) 31
Danté II (robot) 10, **10**
Darkstar, Unmanned Reconnaissance Aerial Vehicle (URAV) 29, **29**
Deep Space 4 (spacecraft) 27, **27**
DENSO 23, **23**
domestic robots 7, **7**, 29, **29**
dwarf robots 16, **17**

E

ELMA (robot) 18-19, **19**
European Space Agency (ESA) 25

F

factories 8, 18, 23, 28
films 6-7, 14-15
fire 9, 10
fire fighting 13, **13**, 31

H

Helpmate 9, **9**
Honda-Sapiens 29, **29**
hospitals 9, 21, 28
humanoid robots 6, **6-7**, 19, **19**, 29, 30, 31
Huygens probe **24**, **26**, 27

I

infrared 16, 29, 30
insects 16, **16**, 18, 28

J

Japan 7, 8, 9, 31
Jason Junior (underwater robot) 12-13, **12-13**

K

Kismet 19, **19**
Knuckles (robotic arm) 13, **13**

M

Manny (robot) 31
manufacturing 8
Mars 6, 24-25
Mars Pathfinder **24**, 25
master-slave robots 14, **14**
medical robots 9, 20-21, **20-21**, 22-23, **22-23**
microspies 28, **28**
military robots 28, 29
miniature technology 16, 22-23, 28, **28**

N

nanorobots 22-23, **22-23**
nanotechnology 23
NASA 10, 24, 27, 30
Neptune (planet) 24
neural networking 17, 30
Nomad rover 24, **24**
nuclear industry 13

O

oceans 6, 12-13, 28

P

Predator (robotic aircraft) 29, **29**
production line 6, 8, **8**

R

radio control 10, 15, 30
remote control 13, 28
Remote Manipulator System (RMS) 24, **24**, 31
Robart III 31
Robbie the Robot 14-15, **15**
Robodoc 20-21, **20-21**
robot aircraft 28-29
robot lawnmower 9, **9**

robot shopping trollies 9, **9**
robot vacuum cleaner 9, **9**
robotic arms 8, 10, **11**, 13, **13**, 20, **20**, 24, 29, 31
robotic farm workers 6, **6**
robotic models 14-15, **14-15**
robotic spacecraft 24, **24**, 25, 26-27, **26-27**
Robotuna 29, **29**
Robug 10, **10**

S

Sarcos 14, **14**
satellites 24, 31
Saturn (planet) 24-25, **24-25**, 26, 27, **27**
sensors 9, 14, 18, 19, 31
smart robots 16, **17**
software 7, 8, 16, 18, 30
Sojourner rover **24**, 25
solar power 9, 16, 25
sonar 12, 30
space probes 10, 24, **24**, 25, 30
space shuttle 24
spider-like robots 10, **10**, 31
Stardust probe 27, **27**
submersibles 12, 13, 30
swarm robots 16, 17, **17**, **18**, 19, **19**

T

telemetry suits 14, **14**
telerobotics 10, 30
Tempel 1 (comet) 24, 27
Titan (moon) 24-25, **24-25**, 26, 27, **27**
toy robots 7, **7**, 28, **28**

U

ultrasound 9, 16, 23, 30, 31
underwater 10, 12-13, **12-13**, 29, 30
US Cybermotion SR2 9, **9**

V

video cameras 10, **10**, 11
virtual reality 20, 29
Voyager probes 24

W

welding 6, 8